Dolphins

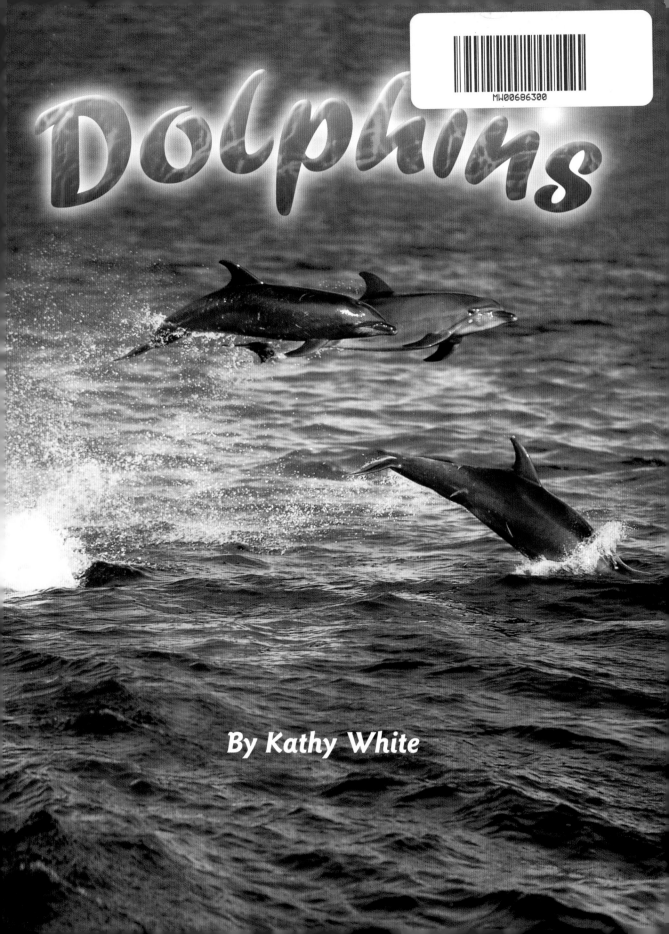

By Kathy White

PM Plus Non Fiction
Ruby

U.S. Edition © 2013 HMH Supplemental Publishers
10801 N. MoPac Expressway
Building #3
Austin, TX 78759
www.hmhsupplemental.com

Text © 2003 Cengage Learning Australia Pty Limited
Illustrations © 2003 Cengage Learning Australia Pty Limited
Originally published in Australia by Cengage Learning Australia

5 6 7 8 9   1957   14
19251

Text: Kathy White
Printed in China by 1010 Printing International Ltd

Acknowledgments
Photographs by AAP Image, p. 29; ANT Photo Library/Barabara Todd, p. 25/K. Griffiths, p. 21 bottom; Australian Picture Library/Corbis/Joel W. Rogers, p. 21 top/Keren Su, p. 27 top/Michael S. Yamashita, p. 20 left/William Boyce, p. 10 bottom/Jeffery L. Rotman, p. 5/Minden Pictures/Flip Nicklin, pp. 9 top, 11 centre, 15 bottom, 16, 11 top/Brandon D. Cole, p. 8 top/Ardea London, p. 8 bottom; Auscape International/Doug Perrine, front cover, pp. 4, 7 left, 9 bottom, 10 top/Francois Gohier, p. 1/Mark Carwardine, p. 12; Digital Vision, p. 20 right; Getty Images/Stone/ Christian Lagereek, p. 14; Lochman Transparencies/Alex Steffe, p. 31, back cover/Len Stewart, p. 21 centre; photolibrary.com/Index Stock/James Watt, p. 11 bottom; PhotoNewZealand.com, p. 7 right; Seapics.com/ Doug Perrine, pp. 13, 15 top/Roland Seitre, p. 27 bottom; Still Pictures/Roland Seitre, p. 30.

Dolphins
ISBN 978 0 75 786913 6

Contents

Introduction

In many ways, dolphins are like humans, which may be why they have interested people for thousands of years. Like people, dolphins live in groups and communicate with each other. They cooperate to find food and when giving birth.

However, sometimes people hurt dolphins by changing the dolphins' environment. Fishing methods and boat traffic have made the oceans, seas, and rivers a more dangerous place for dolphins. Garbage and chemicals are causing water pollution, which destroys the dolphins' habitat. Some kinds of dolphins have become **endangered**.

Today many people know about these problems, and they are trying to protect dolphins. The more we learn about dolphins and their environment, the more we can help them.

Chapter 1

What Are Dolphins?

Dolphins are members of the whale family. There are many different kinds of dolphins. Some live in oceans and seas, while others live in rivers.

All dolphins are mammals. Most mammals, such as humans, dogs, cats, and cattle, live on land. But dolphins live in the sea. Where land mammals have arms and/or legs, dolphins have fins and a tail that propel them through the water.

What are mammals?

Mammals are animals that:
- have strong backbones
- have lungs to breathe air
- give birth to live young
- drink their mother's milk
- are warm-blooded.

Did You Know?

Dolphins have horizontal tails. Fish have vertical tails.

There are differences between dolphins, but most dolphins have these things in common.

The dolphin has a blowhole on the top of its head.

The dolphin uses its **melon** when it sends out sounds.

The dolphin uses its teeth to grab fish, squid, and other prey.

A layer of fat or blubber sits underneath the skin to keep the dolphin warm and **buoyant.**

Fins and flippers help the dolphin steer its body.

The dorsal fin helps the dolphin stay balanced and upright in the water.

The dolphin has a long, strong backbone.

The tail **flukes** move up and down very fast to move the dolphin through the water.

The dolphin is covered in smooth, slippery skin that helps it glide through the water.

Bottlenose Dolphin

Hector's Dolphin

The Bottlenose Dolphin is long and streamlined. Hector's Dolphin is short and stocky. Most dolphins have a sickle-shaped dorsal fin, but others have a rounded dorsal fin.

Kinds of Dolphins

Most kinds of dolphins live in the ocean; some prefer deep waters, and others like shallow coastal areas and harbors. A few kinds of dolphins live in rivers and mangrove swamps.

Pacific White-sided Dolphins live in deep water.

Amazon River Dolphins live in mangrove swamps in Brazil.

Ocean dolphins are divided into two kinds — beaked and non-beaked. Although all dolphins actually have a beak, or snout, some beaks are very short and these dolphins are said to be non-beaked.

Common Dolphins are beaked dolphins.

Risso's Dolphins are non-beaked dolphins.

How to Identify Dolphins

If you are lucky enough to see dolphins, there are a few things to look for that will help you identify them.

Color and markings
Look at the dolphins' colors and markings. Different kinds of dolphins have different markings.

Spotted Dolphins

Pod size
Dolphins swim in groups called **pods**. How big is the pod?
Common Dolphins swim in pods of up to 500.

Location

Where are the dolphins swimming? Some dolphins like warm water, while others like cold water.

Most river dolphins spend their whole lives in fresh water rivers. River dolphins have long beaks and tiny eyes.

Amazon River Dolphin

Speed and style

Some dolphins swim fast and others swim slowly. Some dolphins leap, dive, or spin.

Spinner Dolphin

Dolphin or porpoise?

Porpoises look a lot like dolphins, but they have round heads, small, round bodies, and small triangular fins. They are very shy.

Chapter 2

How Do Dolphins Behave?

Living in Groups

Like many animals, dolphins live in groups for safety reasons. A group provides protection from predators.

A family of dolphins is made up of **dominant** adult male dolphins, some adult female dolphins, some young **calves**, and a few "teenage" dolphins. One or more families make up a pod of dolphins.

Did You Know?

A shark is less likely to attack a dolphin if there are many other dolphins around.

Growing Up

Female dolphins give birth to one calf at a time. A calf is born tail first, and its mother or aunts help to push it to the surface of the water to breathe.

The calf stays close to its mother and drinks her milk for about two years. Calves stay with the pod for many years. Female dolphins sometimes stay with the same pod for their whole life. Adult males often fight for dominance of the pod. The winners get to stay, but the losers have to leave. They may live alone for a while, and then look for a new pod.

Hunting

Dolphins do not rely on their eyes to find food. It is dark underwater, and dolphins do a lot of hunting at night. They use **echolocation** to find prey.

Echolocation is like hearing. Scientists think that dolphins produce **pulses** of sound in their **nasal passages** and send them out through the melon part of their head. When the sound pulses hit a fish, they bounce back like an echo to the dolphin. The echoes tell the dolphin how far away a fish is, what type of fish it is, how fast it is swimming, and the direction that it is going in. The echoes also tell dolphins things like where the coastline or river bank is, and where boats are.

Echolocation gives dolphins a sound map of their environment. They can find things up to one half mile away.

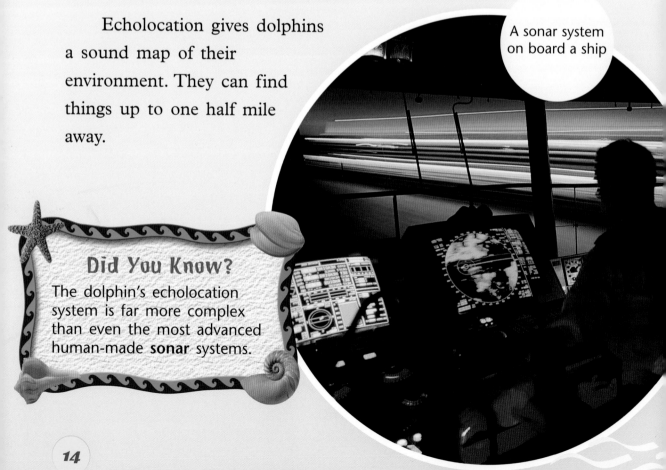

A sonar system on board a ship

Did You Know?

The dolphin's echolocation system is far more complex than even the most advanced human-made **sonar** systems.

Dolphins often hunt together. Some dive below a school of fish to round them up and move them to the surface. Other dolphins wait at the surface to grab the fish with their teeth.

The Tucuxi River Dolphin of Brazil swims sideways and upside down to trap fish against the surface of the water. Then it snaps them up in its long narrow jaws.

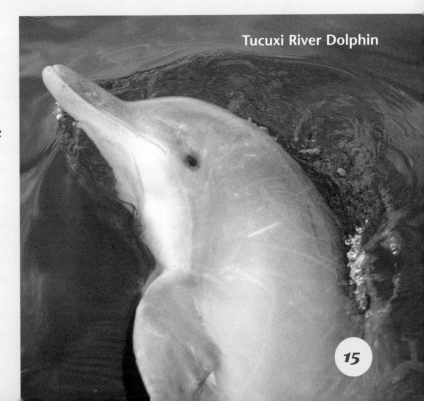

Tucuxi River Dolphin

Whistles, Clicks, and Squeals

Dolphins communicate with each other to find food and to find their way around. They whistle, click, and squeal.

Dolphins make sounds using air. Near a dolphin's blowhole, there are two small tough knobs of tissue called nasal plugs, and some air sacs that collect air. The nasal plugs seal tightly, but when they relax, they let out a pulse of air, which makes the sound.

People have used underwater microphones to record dolphin sounds. What they hear sounds like a busy kitchen, with knives, forks, and plates clinking and rattling. But humans can't hear most dolphin sounds because they are too high-pitched.

Make Dolphin Sounds

You will need a balloon for this experiment. The neck of the balloon is like a dolphin's blowhole.

1 Blow up the balloon, but don't tie it off.

2 Hold the open neck of the balloon and stretch it sideways until it squeals.

3 Stretch the balloon neck more or less tightly. What makes a higher-pitched squeal? By changing the tightness of the balloon neck, you can change the sounds.

Dolphins in the Food Chain

Like many animals, dolphins are part of a food chain.

Killer Whales and sharks hunt and eat small dolphins. However, dolphin pods will attack sharks to drive them away.

Did You Know?

River dolphins have been known to eat small turtles and even birds.

Dolphins feed on squid and fish that are high in fat and protein.

Dolphins sometimes eat crustaceans, such as shrimp and crabs.

Fish, squid, and crustaceans eat plankton. Plant and animal plankton are tiny living things.

Chapter 3

Dangers to Dolphins

Many dangers to dolphins and other **marine** or river animals happen when people change the natural environment.

Some kinds of fishing nets are a danger for marine dolphins.

Drift nets are many miles long and are used in deep waters to catch fish and squid.
The nets hang from floats at the water's surface.
They catch and drown marine mammals such as dolphins.

Did You Know?

Since 1990, the "dolphin safe" tuna program has saved the lives of thousands of dolphins.

Ghost nets are discarded fishing nets that are left in the water. Dolphins and other animals get trapped in the nets.

Purse-shaped nets are used to catch salmon and tuna. Dolphins often swim with these fish and get caught in the nets and drown.

Collisions with boats and ships can injure or kill dolphins, especially in crowded rivers or coastal waters. Water pollution makes dolphins sick and sometimes they die.

Waste water is pumped into the sea.

Chapter 4

Endangered Dolphins

The following four kinds of dolphins are endangered.
They include one marine dolphin and three river dolphins.

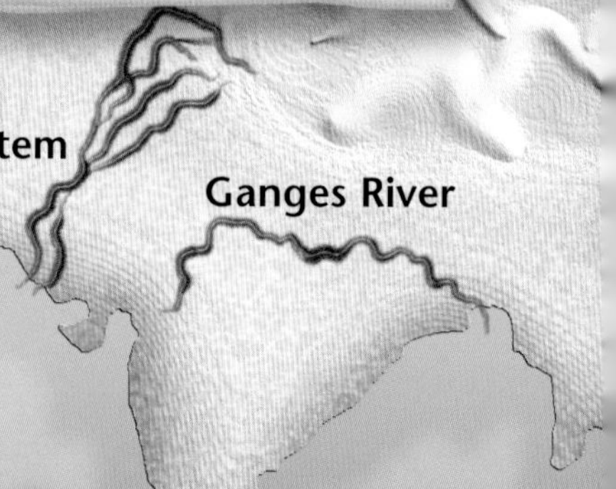

Indus River System

Ganges River

ENDANGERED

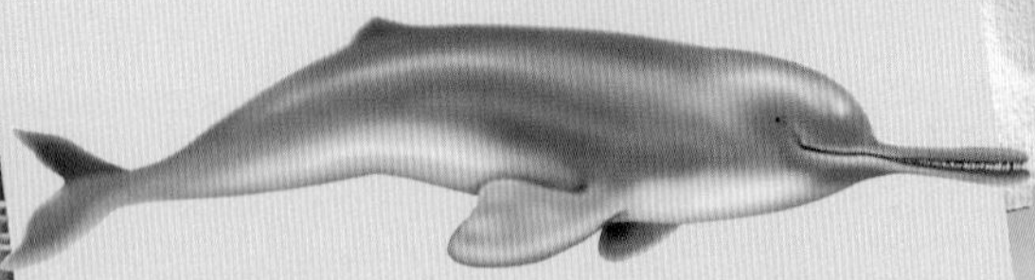

Indus River Dolphin:
- found in the Indus River in Pakistan
- about 950 left

ENDANGERED

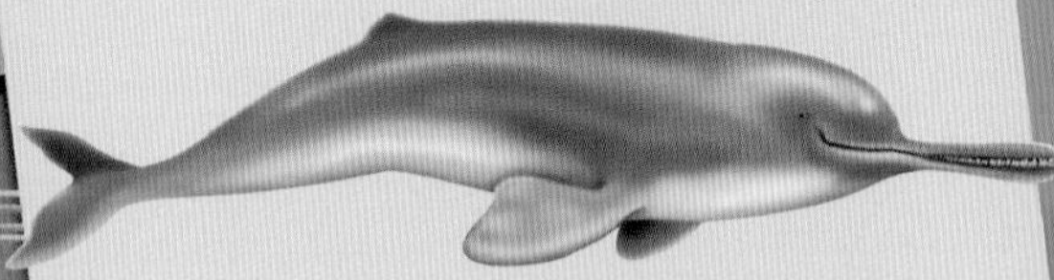

Ganges River Dolphin:
- found in the rivers of India, Bangladesh, Nepal and Bhutan
- 4,000 to 5,000 left

ENDANGERED

The Baiji or Chinese River Dolphin:
- the most endangered dolphin
- found in the Yangtze River, China
- fewer than ten left

Yangtze River

Hector's Dolphin:
- the most endangered marine dolphin
- found in coastal waters around New Zealand
- 4,000 to 5,000 left

Hector's Dolphin

ENDANGERED

ENDANGERED

DESCRIPTION:

- small, stocky body
- rounded dorsal fin
- short beak
- black markings on its dorsal fin

- rounded flippers, flukes, and sides of the head
- creamy white throat and belly
- light gray back and sides

Hector's Dolphin is the only endangered marine dolphin in the world. It is also the smallest marine dolphin at around 52 inches long.

Hector's Dolphin is a fast swimmer that can perform acrobatic movements.

WHY IS IT ENDANGERED?

- *Fishing*: fishing nets set by **commercial** and **recreational** fishermen have killed many dolphins.

- *Pollution*: dangerous chemicals found in New Zealand's coastal waters have reduced the number of calves being born.

WHAT IS BEING DONE?

The New Zealand Government has set up a marine mammal **sanctuary** off the South Island. The Government also wants to ban large fishing nets in areas where Hector's Dolphins are in danger.

ENDANGERI

The Baiji, or Chinese River Dolphin

ENDANGERED

DESCRIPTION:

- long body
- low, triangular dorsal fin
- long, narrow beak that grows longer with age
- large paddle-like flippers

- tiny eyes (almost blind)
- pale bluish gray upper body and sides
- white or grayish-white belly

The Baiji is the most endangered dolphin in the world.

Did You Know?
By the time you read this, the Baiji might be extinct!

The crowded Yangtze River

WHY IS IT ENDANGERED?

- *Habitat destruction*: the Yangtze River is regularly drained for **irrigation**, land **reclamation** projects, and the production of **hydroelectricity**. Baijis now have fewer safe places to live and less food to eat.

- *Fishing*: Baijis have become tangled in nets and hooks, and died.

- *Boat traffic*: propellers on boats have injured and killed Baijis.

- *Pollution*: waste water gets into the river and pollutes the water. Baijis become sick and some die.

WHAT IS BEING DONE?

Baijis are protected by Chinese law, but millions of people use the Yangtze River for food, jobs, and transportation. The Chinese Government has not been able to prevent hazards in much of the river.

The Government has set up sanctuaries as **breeding colonies** for Baijis, until parts of their river habitat can be restored and made safe.

A Baiji in a sanctuary

27

The Ganges and Indus River Dolphins

ENDANGERED

These two kinds of dolphins look the same, but are found in different places.

ENDANGERED

DESCRIPTION:

- long body
- low, triangular hump in place of the dorsal fin
- long, narrow beak
- large teeth
- large paddle-shaped flippers
- tiny eyes (blind)
- gray-brown upper body
- pinkish belly
- often swims on its side

The local people call the Ganges River Dolphin "susu" because it makes a noise like a sneeze as it breathes. The Ganges River Dolphin is blind and often swims with its beak out of the water. It prefers deep water, but can live in water that is only three feet deep.

The Indus River Dolphin is called "Bhulan." It sometimes carries its young on its back, above the surface of the water.

- *Habitat destruction*: dams have been built along the rivers where these dolphins live. The rivers are regularly drained for crop irrigation and the production of hydroelectricity.

ENDANGERED

The dolphins are left stranded when the rivers are drained.

- *Fishing*: dolphins are killed for their oil, which is used in fish bait and traditional medicines.

- *Boat traffic*: cargo ships transport oil and gasoline through a dolphin sanctuary. The extra river traffic and pollution harms all river wildlife, and reduces the amount of food available for the dolphins.

- *Pollution*: people dump garbage and waste water into the rivers.

WHAT IS BEING DONE?

The Indian Government has passed a law protecting Ganges River Dolphins. A dolphin sanctuary was set up in Northern India as a safe area and breeding colony. However, cargo ships continue to pass through on their way to a nearby oil refinery, and local people still use fishing nets that catch dolphins.

ENDANGERED

A Ganges River Dolphin comes into close contact with a person.

A dolphin sanctuary was established in Pakistan as a breeding colony for Indus River Dolphins, but this area has not been protected.

Chapter 5

How Can You Help?

Many people are trying to protect dolphins in their natural habitats. Here are some ways that you can help.

☑ Don't throw garbage into the sea, and pick up any garbage that you see on beaches.

☑ Become a member or volunteer of an organization that aims to protect dolphins.

☑ If you go fishing, make sure that you take all of your fishing gear away with you when you are finished.

☑ Write letters asking governments to protect dolphins.

☑ When buying cans of tuna, check that they are "dolphin-friendly." That means the tuna is caught using methods that don't harm dolphins.

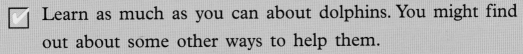

☑ Learn as much as you can about dolphins. You might find out about some other ways to help them.

Glossary

breeding colonies   areas where dolphins give birth and raise their calves

buoyant   floats easily

calves   baby dolphins

commercial   done for a business

dominant   strongest, leading

echolocation   the way dolphins hunt and find things by sending out sounds that come back to them as an echo

endangered   in danger of dying out

flukes   the large, flat, horizontal parts of a dolphin's tail

hydroelectricity   electricity produced from flowing water

irrigation   the moving of water from one place to where it is needed

marine   lives in the sea

melon   the chamber in a dolphin's nose where its sounds are produced

nasal passages   like nostrils in a person's nose

pods   the groups that dolphins swim in

pulses   vibrations

reclamation   the draining and use of land that was underwater, for farming, industry or housing

recreational   done as a hobby

sanctuary   an area where wildlife is protected

sonar   advanced technology used to navigate a ship or boat

territorial waters   the areas of sea near a country that its government can make laws about